LEGENDARY HEROES
OF THE WILD WEST

SACAGAWEA

NATIVE AMERICAN HERO

William R. Sanford &
Carl R. Green

Enslow Publishers, Inc.
44 Fadem Road   PO Box 38
Box 699   Aldershot
Springfield, NJ 07081   Hants GU12 6BP
USA   UK

Library of Congress Cataloging-in-Publication Data

Sanford, William R. (William Reynolds), 1927–
    Sacagawea : Native American hero / William R. Sanford and Carl R. Green.
      p. cm. — (Legendary heroes of the Wild West)
    Includes bibliographical references and index.
    Summary: Profiles the life of the young Shoshoni woman Sacagawea,
who served as an interpreter and guide for the Lewis and Clark expedition at
the beginning of the nineteenth century.
    ISBN 0-89490-675-5
    1. Sacagawea, 1786–1884—Juvenile literature. 2. Shoshoni women—
Biography—Juvenile literature. 3. Lewis and Clark Expedition (1804–1806)—
Juvenile literature. 4. Indians of North America—Biography. [1. Sacagawea,
1786–1884. 2. Shoshoni Indians—Biography. 3. Women—Biography. 4. Lewis and
Clark Expedition (1804–1806)] I. Green, Carl R. II. Title. III. Series: Sanford,
William R. (William Reynolds), 1927– Legendary heroes of the Wild West.
F592.7.S123S47   1997
978'.0049745—dc20
[B]
                               96-269
                               CIP
                               AC

Printed in the United States of America

10 9 8 7 6 5 4 3 2 1

Illustration Credits: American Philosophical Society, p. 34; Denver Public
Library, Western History Collection, p. 6; Montana Historical Society, Helena,
pp. 23, 24; Oregon Department of Transportation, p. 27; William R. Sanford
and Carl R. Green, pp. 11, 19, 38; State Historical Society of North Dakota,
pp. 10, 15, 16, 28, 30, 35; Wyoming Division of Cultural Resources, p. 40.

Cover Illustration: Paul Daly

CONTENTS

AUTHORS' NOTE

In 1804 President Thomas Jefferson ordered Meriwether Lewis and William Clark to explore the American Northwest. On their way west, the explorers hired guides and interpreters. One was a French fur trader named Toussaint Charbonneau. The explorers also obtained the services of Sacagawea, Charbonneau's young Native American wife. It is the brave and resourceful young Shoshone woman who captures our attention today.

Some writers have given Sacagawea credit for guiding Lewis and Clark to the Pacific coast. That was impossible. She had never been west of the Rocky Mountains. Sacagawea did serve as a guide and translator while traveling through regions she knew. Further, when Lewis and Clark met Native American tribes, her presence helped prove that the white men came in peace. These contributions, combined with her wilderness skills, made her a valued member of the expedition.

In many books, writers spell Sacagawea's name with a "j"—Sacajawea. In this book the authors spell her name with a "g." This is the spelling recommended by the Bureau of American Ethnology. However her name is spelled, you are about to read Sacagawea's true story. It is based on the expedition's journals and on Native American oral histories.

1

A JOYFUL REUNION

~~~~~~~~~~~~~~~~~~

In 1805 the United States was looking westward. Two years earlier, President Thomas Jefferson had purchased the Louisiana Territory. The new nation now stretched from the Mississippi River to the Rocky Mountains. Captains Meriwether Lewis and William Clark were pushing deep into the Northwest. Their goal was to open a route to the Pacific.

On August 17, the Corps of Discovery was fifteen months out of St. Louis. It was a crucial time. The Rocky Mountains loomed ahead. Soon their canoes would be useless. Lewis and Clark needed horses. The Shoshone were nearby—and the tribe bred fine horses.

Each Native American tribe raised a new challenge. Some chiefs welcomed the white men. Others treated them as enemies. The captains had less reason to fear the

Sacagawea earned a place for herself in American history by serving as guide, interpreter, and food gatherer for the Lewis and Clark expedition. Because no one in the expedition sketched her likeness, modern artists can only guess at her appearance.

Shoshone than they did other tribes. Traveling with them was a Shoshone woman named Sacagawea. Taken captive as a child, she had grown up in a Hidatsa village far to the east.

Sacagawea's husband, Toussaint Charbonneau, served as an interpreter. He did not speak Shoshone. Lewis and Clark were counting on the young wife and mother to interpret for them. That morning, she was picking berries near the Beaverhead River. Her infant son Pomp rode in a cradleboard on her back.

All at once Sacagawea spotted several Shoshone on horseback. The sight caused her to dance for joy. Turning, she put her fingers in her mouth. Clark read the gesture. It meant that the riders were from her tribe. The return of their long-lost sister amazed the Shoshone. They led the explorers to their camp.

One of the white men described the meeting. As the party neared the camp, "a woman made her way through the crowd toward Sacagawea. . . . Recognizing each other, they embraced with the most tender affection. . . . They had been companions in childhood."[1] Like Sacagawea, Willow Woman had been taken captive. Unlike her friend, she escaped and found her way home.

That afternoon the captains met with Chief Cameahwait. A sail from one of the dugout canoes shaded the men from the sun. The chief seated Clark on a white robe. Then he tied six small shells in Clark's red hair. As a further sign that they met in peace, the men took off their moccasins. A sacred peace pipe passed from hand to hand.

Now it was time to talk. Lewis sent for Sacagawea to interpret. Without her, the council could not proceed. She entered the circle with her eyes cast down as a mark of respect for the tribe's elders. When the captains spoke, Charbonneau repeated their words in Hidatsa. Sacagawea then translated into Shoshone.

Sacagawea sat near Clark. The American made a speech that explained the purpose of his journey. Sacagawea looked up—and recognized the chief. Cameahwait was her older brother! She jumped up and threw her blanket around him. Then she wept as she hugged him. Brother and sister talked briefly. Sacagawea's tears of joy flowed freely as she returned to her seat.

Later, Sacagawea's happiness turned to sorrow. Most of her family was dead. Only Cameahwait and her sister's son had survived. As custom required, Sacagawea adopted the boy. Then she gave him to his uncles to be raised.[2] At that point an older warrior stepped forward. Sacagawea's father, the man claimed, had given her to him in marriage. He dropped his claim when he learned that Pomp was Charbonneau's child.

With Sacagawea's help, Lewis and Clark bought a string of packhorses. On August 27, they gave the command to move out. Sacagawea said farewell to her brother. She never saw him again.

2
A SHOSHONE CHILDHOOD

Sacagawea's long trek into legend began in Idaho's Lemhi River valley. Her father was a chief of the Shoshone. The tribal name means "People who live in the valley." Her year of birth was 1788. No one knows the day or month. It may have been in March, the Moon of the Rushing Waters.[1]

It was common for Native Americans to have more than one name during their lifetimes. Sacagawea's name at birth was Bo-i-naiv (Grass Maiden). The Hidatsa renamed her Sacagawea. That was the name Lewis and Clark knew her by. It translates as Bird Woman. In later years, she was called Lost Woman, Porivo (Chief), and Water White-Man.[2]

The Shoshone wandered north from Mexico hundreds of years before Sacagawea was born. For a time, the tribe lived in the great basin between the Sierra Nevada and the Rocky Mountains. Then came a searing drought. As game animals left the basin, the Shoshone became nomads. Always on the move, they ate salmon, squirrels, rabbits, rats, and lizards. The children gathered roots, seeds, and berries. When hunters came home with empty hands, the women roasted crickets and grasshoppers. Water was scarce. Little could be spared for bathing.

In summer the Shoshone dressed lightly. Men wore a breechcloth of badger hide. Women wore a leather apron.

In this Karl Bodmer engraving, a tribe has set up a tipi village on the edge of the Great Plains. In a scene typical of Shoshone tribal life, a woman occupies herself with her daily chores. On the far side of the tipi, her husband plans the day's hunt with a fellow warrior.

By the mid-1700s the Shoshone were ranging far out on the plains in search of buffalo. In this dramatic engraving, a hunter signals that he has located a herd. After eating or preserving the meat, the tribe used the hides for teepees and blankets, the bones for weapons and tools, and the sinews for bowstrings.

Men and women walked the rocky trails in yucca fiber sandals. Their homes were crude brush shelters called wickiups. When winter swept the basin, the Shoshone put on leggings, moccasins, and rabbit-fur capes.

By the late 1700s some Shoshone bands had moved into the mountains. Sacagawea's people were one of these Plateau tribes. Fur traders who found them living near the Snake River called them the Snake people. The climate was harsh, but there was water and game. Shoshone hunters killed deer, bear, sheep, beavers, and ducks with arrows and spears. Buckskin shirts and tunics became common. In time some of the Shoshone found their way eastward to the Great Plains. The hunting was better there. One buffalo could feed an entire band.

Buffalo hunts brought the Shoshone into contact with the Plains tribes. With no language in common, the hunters talked in sign language. The Shoshone way of life began to change. Wickiups gave way to tipis made of buffalo hides. When the tribe moved, the people dragged their tipis with them. By the 1740s the Shoshone were trading beaver pelts for handsome spotted horses. Hunters ranged far out on the plains in search of buffalo.[3]

This was the world that Sacagawea knew as a child. Her two brothers were trained to be hunters and warriors. She and her sister were taught to gather food, cook, sew, and care for babies. Sacagawea learned how to find over a hundred edible plants. One of her favorites was the camas lily. The Shoshone dried the potatolike bulbs and ate them.

Sacagawea's mother showed her how to cook a favorite dish. She used flat stones to grind acorns, nuts, and seeds into a meal. Then she filled a large yucca basket with water, meal, and chunks of meat. A coating of pitch made the basket waterproof. To cook the stew, Sacagawea dropped hot stones from the campfire into the basket. The family ate the thick, tasty stew by dipping their fingers into the basket.

The Shoshone hunted buffalo with bows and arrows. Some rival Plains tribes had traded with white men for rifles. As the Shoshone pushed into their hunting grounds, these tribes pushed back. Peaceful contacts gave way to bloody hit-and-run raids. It was one of these raids that changed the course of Sacagawea's life.

3
CAPTURED BY
HIDATSA RAIDERS

Sometime around 1800, Sacagawea's father called for a summer hunt. His plan was to join other Shoshone at the three forks of the Missouri River. On today's maps, the site lies in western Montana. All the children knew the importance of the hunt. They would go hungry that winter if it failed.

Sacagawea rose at dawn with the rest of the band. The first job was to pack the family's belongings. Busy hands folded the tipi's hides and poles into a V-shaped frame. Tied behind one of the horses and loaded with bundles, the frame served as a travois. For the next three days, the twelve-year-old walked beside the heavily loaded travois. Only the men rode horseback.

The land of the three forks made a fine campsite. Snowcapped peaks towered over the valley. Beyond lay the plains and the buffalo herds. It was a peaceful scene, but the Shoshone were watchful. They knew that the warlike Hidatsa might ride out of the east at any time. Raiders would be seeking more than horses and scalps. They would try to steal women and children as well.

Sacagawea's band met old friends at the forks. Lines of tipis soon dotted the riverbank. Scouts returned with word that buffalo were grazing nearby. The hunters mounted packhorses and galloped off. Each man led a second horse. These were the faster buffalo horses used in the hunt.

That afternoon, Sacagawea's brother Cameahwait rode back with good news. The hunters had driven some buffalo over a cliff. Sacagawea and the other women hurried to the spot. First they skinned the dead animals with sharp flint knives. Next, they hacked the flesh into smaller pieces and piled them on a travois. Horses dragged the meat and hides back to camp. That night, the Shoshone feasted on slabs of roasted hump meat. The women cut the rest of the meat into strips. When laid in the sun, the strips would dry into a long-lasting food (today it is known as jerky). The dried meat was tough, but it was an important part of the winter diet.[1]

The women had to scrape the fat from the hides before they could be tanned. Sacagawea took her turn with the scraper the next morning. It was hot, tiring work. In the afternoon she joined the other girls by the river. As they chatted, a burst of gunfire shattered the quiet. The girls saw a band of Hidatsa warriors riding into the camp. Most of the Shoshone men were out hunting. Those who were left knew their bows were no match for rifles. The men scattered. The women grabbed their children and fled.

Sacagawea tried to find a hiding place. A thick grove of trees on the far side of the river caught her eye. She ran into the river, the icy current tugging at her legs. Her feet slipped on the rocks. Behind her, a horse splashed into the river. A moment later a strong arm plucked her from the water. Sacagawea struggled, but the warrior held her fast.[2]

The Hidatsa fired at anything that moved. Four men, four women, and several boys soon lay dead or dying.[3] As fruits of their success, the raiders carried off Shoshone horses and captives. Their route home followed the Yellowstone River, then the Missouri.

At times Sacagawea's captor allowed her to ride. More often she and the other captives were forced

In this old engraving, the artist portrayed a Hidatsa tribal leader in full ceremonial dress. To earn status in the tribe, young men joined raiding parties in hopes of seizing horses and women. It was during one of these raids that Red Arrow captured Sacagawea and took her back to his village.

to walk. Soon the mountains faded from sight. Blowing sand stung their faces. Only sagebrush and tumbleweeds grew in the gray alkaline soil. Farther east, a sea of prairie grass stretched to the horizon.

At last the Hidatsa reached their village on the Knife River. The city of Bismarck, North Dakota, would one day take root on the site. Sacagawea had never before seen a village circled by a wall of logs. Inside the wall, the Hidatsa lived in round, earth-covered lodges. The gates swung open as the raiding party drew near. Tied to the back of a horse, Sacagawea rode toward an uncertain future.

Unlike the Shoshone, the Hidatsa lived in round, earth-covered lodges. After her capture, Sacagawea lived and worked in a village like this one. Here, the village serves as a backdrop for the first meeting of Sacagawea, Charbonneau, and the men of the Lewis and Clark expedition.

4

FOREST BEAR AND LITTLE CHIEF

Unlike the Shoshone, the Hidatsa were farmers as well as hunters. With food crops to cultivate, they lived year-round in their villages. Inside each round lodge, the floor lay a foot or more below ground level. The step-down floors and thick walls kept the lodges cool in summer and warm in winter.[1]

Sacagawea's captor, a man named Red Arrow, put her to work in the fields. Each day she tended the maize, squash, and beans. To hoe the maize, she used a tool made from a buffalo's shoulder bone. At harvest time, she stacked the ears on a platform to dry. Later, the Hidatsa beat the ears with sticks to free the kernels.

A year or two passed. Then, one winter's night, Sacagawea's life changed again. Like many Hidatsa warriors, Red Arrow liked to gamble. The game he played was a simple one. First, the players made their bets. Next, a "dealer" hid a pebble under one of four moccasins. Guessing wrong cost the player his bet—a fur, some beads, or a knife. One night Red Arrow lost a bet with Toussaint Charbonneau. Pulling Sacagawea to her feet, Red Arrow pushed her toward the French Canadian fur trader. He had bet her against the trader's buffalo horse.[2]

Charbonneau made Sacagawea his third wife. One of the older wives was a Hidatsa woman. The other was a Shoshone named Otter Woman. Charbonneau was thirty years older than Sacagawea. The Hidatsa said he was slow-witted and clumsy. They called him Forest Bear.[3] His fellow fur traders said he was a sneak and a scoundrel.

In the spring of 1804, Sacagawea became pregnant. As the months passed, she made fur-lined clothing for the baby. One day that fall, Charbonneau rushed in with amazing news. In Hidatsa, he told her that white men had been seen on the river.

Down at the riverbank, Sacagawea caught her first glimpse of the strangers. She stared at their blue uniforms and pale skins. In time she met the two leaders. The blond, silent man was Captain Meriwether Lewis. The cheerful redhead was Captain William Clark. Clark never did learn to pronounce her name. He called her Janey.

The explorers were sailing upriver in three boats. The largest was a keelboat with a cannon mounted at each end. The two smaller boats were canoe-shaped dugouts called pirogues. The white men landed and pitched tents near the

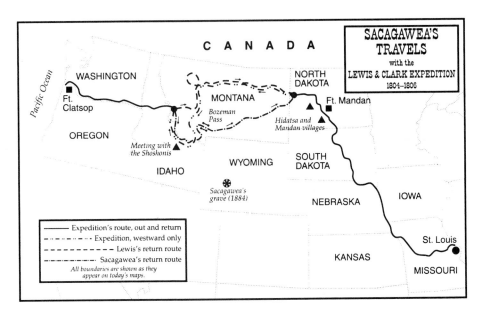

Lewis and Clark sailed up the Missouri River on the first leg of their epic journey to the Pacific. At Fort Mandan in North Dakota they acquired the services of a French interpreter and his Shoshone wife, Sacagawea. The route west then took the expedition across the Rocky Mountains to the Pacific coast. On the return journey, Lewis and Clark split up and took separate routes across Montana.

river. A lively trading session followed. The Hidatsa and their Mandan neighbors bartered cornmeal and furs for medals and tobacco.

The chiefs allowed the captains to build a winter camp. Sacagawea marveled at the speed with which the soldiers' axes felled trees. A log fort soon rose on the site. Lewis and Clark named it Fort Mandan. When they needed an interpreter, they hired Charbonneau.

Village gossip told Sacagawea more about the white

men. Their chief was President Thomas Jefferson. He had purchased a vast tract of land from a country called France. This Louisiana Territory included the lands of the Hidatsa and Mandan. Now Jefferson wanted to know more about the land. What grew there? Who lived there? Was there an easy route through the mountains to the great western sea?

Charbonneau saw a chance to make some money. He offered to go with Lewis and Clark when they paddled up the Missouri in the spring. When they reached the land of the Shoshone, he and Sacagawea could interpret. It was a good argument. The captains would have to trade for Shoshone horses when they left the river.

On February 11, 1805, Sacagawea gave birth to a son. A friend gave her a tonic to make the birth easier. The drink was made of crushed rattlesnake rattles. Charbonneau named the boy Jean Baptiste. Around the camp he was called Pomp. In Shoshone, the nickname meant First Born, or Little Chief.

By March, Sacagawea was strong again. Pomp was thriving and the weather was good. The captains gave the orders to prepare for the trip westward.

5

A PERILOUS
JOURNEY

On April 7, Lewis and Clark left Fort Mandan. Their party included twenty-seven soldiers, two interpreters, Sacagawea, and Pomp. All embarked in two pirogues and six small canoes. Lewis felt the thrill of heading into the unknown. In his journal he compared his tiny fleet to the ships Columbus sailed to the New World.[1]

To escape the crowded pirogue, Sacagawea often trekked along the riverbanks. Walking gave her a chance to gather plants. Wild onions, berries, plums, and Jerusalem artichokes found their way onto the camp menu. At night Sacagawea and Pomp shared the one tent with Charbonneau and the two captains.

The men survived run-ins with bears and rattlesnakes. It was the river that caused the most trouble. On May 14, a wind gust tipped the lead pirogue on its side. The boat righted itself, but much of the cargo spilled out. As the men paddled for shore, Sacagawea calmly retrieved the floating bundles. Her quick thinking saved journals, scientific instruments, and medicines. A few days later Lewis and Clark named a waterway in her honor. The stream they called Bird Woman's River is known today as Crooked Creek.[2]

On June 10, Sacagawea fell ill. Puzzled by her symptoms, Clark tried bleeding her. Then he dosed her with laudanum and applied pine bark poultices. A check of her pulse led Lewis to fear for her life. He added mineral water to the treatment. The pungent drink seemed to help. By June 17, his patient was sipping soup. On the day her appetite came back, she ate too many green apples. That night the pain and fever returned. Lewis scolded Charbonneau for not taking care of her. By the next day, however, Sacagawea felt well enough to go fishing.

The next near-disaster struck a few days later. To escape a hailstorm, Clark led Sacagawea and Pomp to shelter under a rock ledge. All at once a wall of water surged through the canyon. Sacagawea grabbed Pomp just as the flash flood carried off his cradleboard. Clark then pushed mother and son up the steep hillside to safety.

One day Sacagawea saw trees that had been stripped of their edible bark. It was a sign that she was nearing the land of the Shoshone. In July, she found the spot where she had been captured. Two weeks later, she danced for joy to see her people again.

The sight of the Three Forks of the Missouri warned Lewis and Clark that they were nearing the Rocky Mountains. From this point onward, the explorers looked for signs of Sacagawea's tribe, the Shoshone. Lewis wrote, "If we do not find them or some other nation who have horses I fear the successful[l] issue of our voyage will be very doubtful[l]."

Riding Shoshone horses over Shoshone land, the explorers pushed westward. The Lolo Trail led them into the land of the Nez Percé. At first, the Nez Percé feared that the white men would attack them. The sight of Sacagawea and Pomp eased their fears. War parties did not travel with women and children. The tribe fed the strangers and provided guides.

The expedition crossed the Great Divide in knee-deep snow. Next came the Clearwater River. This was a milestone. Rivers now flowed west instead of east. The Nez Percé guides described a river route that followed the Clearwater to the Snake. The Snake, in turn, flowed into the Columbia. It was the Columbia that would carry them to the sea. Before leaving in dugout canoes, the men buried their extra supplies. The Nez Percé promised to care for the horses.

In October, Lewis and Clark headed their canoes downriver. Food was scarce. The men butchered dogs and horses for food. Tribal customs kept Sacagawea from eating the meat. She lived on fish, plants, and roots until Lewis bagged some ducks.

The Columbia came into view on October 16. Lewis and Clark hoped for an easy passage, but the great river defied them. The men had to carry their canoes and supplies around rapids and waterfalls. Rain fell almost daily. Clothing and bedding rotted.

On November 7, Sacagawea heard the roar of breaking waves. The explorers were certain they had reached the ocean. "O the joy!" Clark wrote. "The cheering view exhilarated the spirits of all the party."[3]

The sight of Sacagawea (kneeling beside Lewis and Clark) helped convince the Plains tribes that the explorers came in peace. Western artist Charles Russell captured one of those moments in this splendid work, "Lewis and Clark meeting Indians at Ross's Hole." The mural can be seen in Montana's State Capitol Building in Helena.

6

A DREARY WINTER ON THE PACIFIC COAST

The explorers soon discovered their mistake. What looked like the ocean was only the wide mouth of the Columbia. Sacagawea and some of the men became seasick as waves tossed the canoes. Lewis and Clark beached the canoes at Point Ellice, twenty miles from the ocean. Fog and rain further dampened the men's spirits. They lived on dried fish and roots supplied by the local Chinook tribe.[1]

Clark wanted to go upriver to find a dry campsite. Lewis argued that they should spend the winter on the coast. If a ship came by, he wanted to buy medicines and other supplies. They might even book passage and sail home in comfort.[2]

Scouts found good hunting on the south side of the river. On December 5, Lewis picked a site a few miles inland for a winter camp. The spot lay on high ground amid a grove of tall fir trees. A spring flowed nearby. Sacagawea voted with the others to approve the choice. Anxious to escape the rain, the men started work on Fort Clatsop. The name paid tribute to people from the Clatsop tribe who brought gifts of food.

Eight cabins with sloping roofs rose on the site. Douglas firs yielded fine boards two feet in width. Work crews also salvaged lumber from an old Chinook village. A stout log stockade completed the defenses. On Christmas Eve, Sacagawea, Charbonneau, and Pomp moved into a room of their own.

The men observed Christmas with songs and a loud chorus of rifle fire. Sacagawea gave Clark two dozen white weasel tails. The Shoshone prized the tails for their beauty. The Christmas feast featured elk meat (spoiled) and roast wapato roots (delicious). Sacagawea was fond of this pota-tolike food.

By the next day the men were back at work. There was furniture to build and clothing to mend. Hunting parties stalked elk, deer, beaver, and sea otter. Sacagawea helped sew moccasins and shirts from the hides. By boiling sea water, the men made four quarts of "white, fine" salt a day.[3] The cooks used the salt for flavoring and to preserve meat.

The constant rain shrouded the fort in gloom. The men suffered from colds, flu, boils, and lumbago. Fleas infested the camp. Sentries stood guard to keep the Chinook from stealing tools and supplies. Lewis and Clark preferred the

This sunlit mural depicts the expedition's arrival at the mouth of the Columbia. In real life, rain and fog dampened spirits, food was scarce, and everyone's clothing was in rags. Eager to find shelter, Lewis picked a winter campsite on the south side of the river.

Clatsop. Sacagawea spoke in sign language to Chief Comowoll when he came to trade.

On January 5, the Clatsop brought news of a beached whale. As Clark made plans to visit the site, Sacagawea asked for a favor. Lewis reported her request in these words: "The poor woman stated . . . that she had traveled a great way with us to see the great water, yet she had never been down to the coast. Now that this monstrous fish was also to be seen, it seemed hard that she should be permitted to see neither the ocean nor the whale."[4]

Two days later, Sacagawea stood on a bluff above the Pacific. The "great water" looked as though it stretched to the edge of the world. She lifted eleven-month-old Pomp so he could see waves crash on the sand. By that time the Clatsop had stripped the great "fish" of blubber. When

Sacagawea reached the beach, she marveled at the immense bones. Clark measured the whale's length at 105 feet.

As the weeks passed, hopes of meeting a supply ship died. Lewis and Clark worked on their notes and planned the return trip. Lewis traded his gold-laced coat for a canoe. As a good-bye gift, the captains gave Fort Clatsop to Chief Comowoll.

The skies cleared at midday on March 23. Sacagawea took a seat in one of the canoes. The dugouts moved slowly up the river as the men bent to their paddles.

Fort Mandan (shown here), was the model on which Lewis and Clark built their fort near the shores of the Pacific. Sacagawea, Pomp, and the men of the expedition celebrated Christmas, 1805, within the friendly walls of Fort Clatsop. The snug, eight-cabin enclosure was named for a tribe that lived nearby.

7

THE RETURN TRIP

~~~~~~~~~~~~~~~~~~~~~~

The hunting was good along the Columbia that spring of 1806. By early April the party had salted down a good supply of meat. Most of the Native Americans the explorers met were friendly. A few turned out to be thieves. Lewis had to send three armed men to recover his guard dog, Scannon.[1]

Swift currents forced Lewis and Clark to abandon their canoes. Once again they needed horses. Once again Sacagawea helped buy them. This time the Walla Walla tribe furnished the packhorses. To prove his friendship, Chief Yellept gave Clark a fine white horse. Clark, not to be outdone, gave Yellept his sword.

The expedition reached the Nez Percé in early May. In one village an old man was saying that the white men had come to kill his people. Sacagawea found a visiting

Shoshone who spoke the Nez Percé language. Through him, she convinced the chiefs that Lewis and Clark had come in peace. Clark further won the tribe's trust with his self-taught doctoring skills. He treated wounds, set broken bones, and washed out sore eyes.

Clark's skills were sorely tested by Pomp's illness late in May. At almost fourteen months, Pomp was cutting teeth. To add to his discomfort, he developed a high fever, a swollen neck, and diarrhea. The two captains worried about him. Lewis wrote on May 24, "The child was very

In addition to their skills as woodsmen and mapmakers, William Clark (left) and Meriwether Lewis were excellent naturalists. They kept careful notes on the people, animals, and plants of the vast region. Lewis died in 1809, but Clark lived long enough to begin a new career as the nation's Superintendent of Indian Affairs.

wrestless [sic] last night. [Its] jaw and the back of [its] neck are much more swol[l]en than they were yesterday."[2] Clark treated the diarrhea with cream of tartar. Then he applied a poultice of hot onions to the boy's neck. Later, he switched to a salve made of pine resin, beeswax, and bear's oil. By early June, Pomp was his happy self again.

The men's all-meat diet left them with headaches and stomachaches. Sacagawea's knowledge of wild plants helped relieve the symptoms. A trip through the woods produced fennel (a carrotlike root) and wild onions. The flavor of the horse and dog stew improved—and so did the men's health.

Lewis and Clark split the party after crossing the Rockies. Lewis turned north, hoping to find a shorter route to the Great Falls. Clark headed south along the Yellowstone River. The plan called for them to meet where the Yellowstone joins the Missouri. Sacagawea, Pomp, and Charbonneau went with Clark.

For a time, Clark followed a well-traveled trail. All went well until he reached the plains. There the trail branched in many directions. Sacagawea stepped forward. Her people once had come here to dig camas roots, she said. She told Clark to head for the highest part of the plain. From there he would see a gap in the mountains. Crossing that gap, she promised, would lead them to where their supplies were hidden.

Clark followed her advice. On July 8, the party reached the Jefferson River and the cache of supplies. A few days later Sacagawea again pointed the way. As they neared the Yellowstone River, Clark saw two passes ahead. He wrote, "[Sacagawea] has been of great service to me as a pilot through this country. [She] recommends a gap in the mountains more south which I shall cross."[3] Today, that gap is known as the Bozeman Pass.

The weather was cold enough to leave a skin of ice on standing water. It was not cold enough to drive off the mosquitoes. Swarms of the pesky insects sometimes kept hunters from aiming their rifles. On the south side of the Yellowstone, Clark climbed a two-hundred-foot pillar of rock. With little Pomp in mind, he named it Pompy's Tower. Today it is known as Pompey's Pillar.

Clark and his party met Lewis and his men two weeks later. Now it was time for the party to paddle down the Missouri. On August 14, 1806, they sighted a Mandan village. Crowds turned out to watch their progress. Soon the Hidatsa villages came into view. Sacagawea was home again.

8

HOMECOMING

No record exists of Sacagawea's homecoming. We can guess that the women treated her with respect. She had been little more than a girl when she left. Now, eighteen months later, she returned a strong, confident woman. Her baby had grown into an active, handsome child. Most of all, Sacagawea had played a major role in the expedition's success.[1]

Clark had grown quite fond of Pomp. He wrote, "I offered to take [her] little son, a beautiful promising child who is 19 months old." The offer was well meant, but Pomp had not been weaned. Charbonneau asked Clark to wait a year. Clark agreed, and promised to raise Pomp in "such a manner as I thought proper."[2]

Fire had destroyed Fort Mandan. Lewis and Clark set up camp near a Mandan village. They urged the Mandan

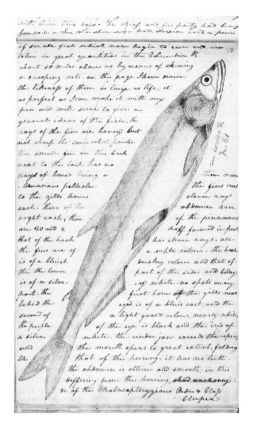

and Hidatsa chiefs to visit St. Louis. In the end, only one chief agreed. The others feared the passage through the lands of the Sioux. Their refusal meant that Charbonneau was no longer needed to interpret.

Clark gave Charbonneau $500.33. The money paid for his services as an interpreter and for his horse and tent. If Sacagawea received any pay, it was not recorded. Clark did pay her tribute in his journal. "[Sacagawea] was particularly useful among the Shoshone. Indeed, she had borne with a patience truly admirable the fatigues of so long a route encumbered with the charge of an infant."[3]

Three days later the captains said their good-byes and headed downstream. On August 20, Clark wrote to Sacagawea and Charbonneau. His letter renewed his offer to raise Pomp. He called the child his "little dancing boy."

Clark added, "If you wish to live with the white people, and will come to me, I will give you a piece of land . . . horses, cows and hogs."[4]

Charbonneau did take Sacagawea and Pomp to St. Louis that fall. He also took Otter Woman, his second Shoshone wife. She was older than Sacagawea, and her son, Toussaint, was older than Pomp. Charbonneau spent the next few years in the woods. In October 1810 he bought the farmland Clark had offered him. A few months later he sold the land back to Clark for $100. The fur trader had tired quickly of life as a farmer.

In 1811 Charbonneau traveled upriver with lawyer Henry Brackenridge. The fur trader had only one of his wives with him. He left his sons behind in St. Louis, where Clark acted as their

Lewis and Clark were well aware of Sacagawea's contributions to their success. Many years passed, however, before the nation recognized her role in the opening of the West. In 1910 the people of Bismarck, North Dakota, paid tribute to Sacagawea and little Pomp by erecting this bronze statue.

guardian. Meriwether Lewis had died in 1809. Clark was carving out a new career as Superintendent of Indian Affairs.

Brackenridge wrote, "We have on board a Frenchman named Chabonet [sic], with his wife, . . . both of whom accompanied Lewis and Clark to the Pacific. . . . The woman [is] a good creature of mild and gentle disposition. [She] was greatly attracted to whites, whose manners and airs she tries to imitate. . . . She longed to revisit her native country."[5] As often happened when whites wrote about Native American women, he did not use Sacagawea's name.

War with Great Britain broke out in the spring of 1812. The threat from Canada alarmed a rich fur trader named Manuel Lisa. Lisa ordered his men to build Fort Manuel on the northern border of South Dakota. Charbonneau was part of the work crew. John Luttig was one of the clerks.

On December 20, Luttig wrote, "This evening the wife of Charbonneau . . . died of a putrid fever. She was . . . the best woman in the fort, aged about 25 years. She left a fine infant girl."[6]

Luttig did not record the name of the woman who died. When Clark read the report, he assumed she was Sacagawea. Was this the end of the Bird Woman's story?

9

A LASTING LEGACY

As the nation moved westward, few stopped to think about Sacagawea. Decades passed before interest was reborn. In the 1920s, the Bureau of Indian Affairs sent Charles Eastman to look into the Bird Woman's life. Historian Grace Hebard used Eastman's report in her 1932 book, *Sacajawea*. Hebard and Eastman agreed that "the wife of Charbonneau" who died in 1812 was Otter Woman. Sacagawea, they claimed, lived another seventy-two years.

Hebard and Eastman talked to people who had known the Bird Woman. Around 1820, they wrote, Charbonneau and Sacagawea were out west trapping beaver. Problems cropped up when Charbonneau married a pretty Ute. Sacagawea disliked the new wife. When the women quarreled, Charbonneau took the Ute's side. One day he beat

Sacagawea in front of her. It was not the first beating, but this time Sacagawea packed up and left. After months of wandering, she settled with the Comanches. Their language was a close kin to her native tongue.

Sacagawea married a Comanche. As the years passed she gave birth to five more children. Only a son and a daughter survived. After her husband died in battle, Sacagawea decided to rejoin her own people. When she slipped away, her son Ticannaf led a fruitless search for her. The Comanche began to call her Wadze-wipe, the Lost Woman.[1]

No one knows the route Sacagawea took. She may have joined explorer John Charles Frémont's second expedition. In 1843, Frémont wrote, "An Indian woman of the Snake

nation, desirous . . . to return to her people, . . . obtained permission to travel with my party."[2]

The woman, who was not named, left Frémont at Fort Bridger in Wyoming.

Ample evidence exists to prove that Sacagawea did not die in 1812. More likely, she left Charbonneau and went to live with the Comanches (as pictured here). After her Comanche husband died in battle, she left her adopted people and returned to the Shoshone.

Was she Sacagawea? The meeting with Frémont may be a clue. In that age, only a handful of Native American women had the self-confidence to speak as equals with white men.

Sacagawea's travels in the years that follow are hard to pin down. One report has her moving from Canada to Arizona to California. The next hard evidence comes from the 1860s. During that decade Sacagawea returned to Wyoming and the Shoshone. Her adopted son Bazil gave her a warm welcome. Government agents used her as an interpreter. Agent James Patten was still living in 1926. He confirmed that Sacagawea lived with the Shoshone in the 1870s.[3]

Sacagawea urged the tribe to take up farming. The buffalo, elk, and deer would soon be gone, she warned. When tribal councils met, Sacagawea's words carried great weight. At one council she urged a move to a reservation in the Wind River Mountains. Her people called her Porivo (Chief) because the whites showed her respect.

Sacagawea sometimes wore a medal Clark had given her. She liked to tell the story of the time she fed dog meat to hungry white men. Her great-grandson remembered her as "very old, but bright and gay."[4] When she died, mourners wrapped her in skins. A favorite horse carried her body to the graveyard. Bazil put a small wooden marker at the site. When that vanished, the family marked the grave with small boulders. Today, a fine gravestone stands guard. It reads:

SACAJAWEA
DIED APRIL 9, 1884
A GUIDE WITH THE
LEWIS AND CLARK
EXPEDITION
1805–1806

There are more monuments dedicated to Sacagawea than to any other American woman.[5] Statues and markers can be found from St. Louis to Portland, Oregon. In Montana, Sacagawea Peak overlooks the rivers she traveled. Washington state is home to Sacajawea State Park and Lake Sacajawea. Each tribute adds to the legend of the brave Shoshone woman who helped blaze the trail west.

Shoshone tribal tradition tells us that Sacagawea returned to her people sometime during the 1860s. The tribe knew of her travels with Lewis and Clark, and treated her with respect. When she died, her family buried her with great ceremony. Today, a fine granite tombstone marks the site.

CHAPTER NOTES

Chapter 1

1. Bernard DeVoto, ed., *The Journals of Lewis and Clark* (Boston: Houghton Mifflin Company, 1953), pp. 202–203.

2. Ella E. Clark and Margot Edmond, *Sacagawea of the Lewis and Clark Expedition* (Berkeley: University of California Press, 1979), p. 29.

Chapter 2

1. Jerry Seibert, *Sacajawea: Guide to Lewis and Clark* (Boston: Houghton Mifflin Company, 1960), p. 7.

2. Harold P. Howard, *Sacajawea* (Norman, Okla.: University of Oklahoma Press, 1971), pp. 180–181.

3. Oliver LaFarge, *A Pictorial History of the American Indian* (New York: Crown Publishers, 1956), p. 182.

Chapter 3

1. Oliver LaFarge, *A Pictorial History of the American Indian* (New York: Crown Publishers, 1956), pp. 148–149.

2. James Willard Schultz, *Bird Woman (Sacajawea), the Guide of Lewis and Clark* (Boston: Houghton Mifflin Company, 1918), p. 72.

3. Bernard DeVoto, ed., *The Journals of Lewis and Clark* (Boston: Houghton Mifflin Company, 1953), p. 171.

Chapter 4

1. Harold P. Howard, *Sacajawea* (Norman, Okla.: University of Oklahoma Press, 1971), p. 10.

2. Charles G. Clarke, *The Men of the Lewis and Clark Expedition* (Glendale, Calif.: Arthur H. Clark Company, 1970), pp. 147–148.

3. Betty Skold, *Sacagawea: The Story of an American Indian* (Minneapolis: Dillon Press, 1977), p. 20.

Chapter 5

1. Bernard DeVoto, ed., *The Journals of Lewis and Clark* (Boston: Houghton Mifflin Company, 1953), p. 92.
2. Harold P. Howard, *Sacajawea* (Norman, Okla.: University of Oklahoma Press, 1971), pp. 32–33.
3. Ella E. Clark and Margot Edmond, *Sacagawea of the Lewis and Clark Expedition* (Berkeley: University of California Press, 1979), p. 48.

Chapter 6

1. Delia G. Emmons, *Sacajawea of the Shoshones* (Portland, Ore.: Binford and Mort, 1943), p. 244.
2. Robert G. Ferris, ed., *Lewis and Clark* (Washington, D.C.: United States Department of the Interior, National Park Service, 1975), p. 189.
3. Ella E. Clark and Margot Edmond, *Sacagawea of the Lewis and Clark Expedition* (Berkeley: University of California Press, 1979), p. 54.
4. James Willard Schultz, *Bird Woman (Sacajawea), the Guide of Lewis and Clark* (Boston: Houghton Mifflin Company, 1918), pp. 233–234.

Chapter 7

1. Ella E. Clark and Margot Edmond, *Sacagawea of the Lewis and Clark Expedition* (Berkeley: University of California Press, 1979), pp. 60–61.
2. Bernard DeVoto, ed., *The Journals of Lewis and Clark* (Boston: Houghton Mifflin Company, 1953), p. 391.
3. Grace R. Hebard, *Sacajawea* (Glendale, Calif.: Arthur H. Clark Company, 1957), p. 71.

Chapter 8

1. Olive Burt, *Sacajawea* (New York: Franklin Watts, 1978), p. 35.
2. Bernard DeVoto, ed., *The Journals of Lewis and Clark* (Boston: Houghton Mifflin Company, 1953), p. 458.
3. Ella E. Clark and Margot Edmond, *Sacagawea of the Lewis and Clark Expedition* (Berkeley: University of California Press, 1979), p. 82.

4. Grace R. Hebard, *Sacajawea* (Glendale, Calif.: Arthur H. Clark Company, 1957), pp. 83–84.

5. Harold P. Howard, *Sacajawea* (Norman, Okla.: University of Oklahoma Press, 1971), p. 157.

6. Ibid., p. 160.

Chapter 9

1. Harold P. Howard, *Sacajawea* (Norman, Okla.: University of Oklahoma Press, 1971), pp. 176–177.

2. Ibid., p. 177.

3. Grace R. Hebard, *Sacajawea* (Glendale, Calif.: Arthur H. Clark Company, 1957), p. 227.

4. Ella E. Clark and Margot Edmond, *Sacagawea of the Lewis and Clark Expedition* (Berkeley: University of California Press, 1979), p. 126.

5. "Sacajawea," *Colliers Encyclopedia* (New York: Macmillan Educational Company, 1991), vol. 20, p. 318.

GLOSSARY

bleeding—An outmoded medical technique that treated illness by draining blood from a patient's veins.

blubber—The thick layer of fat found between the skin and muscle layers of whales and other marine mammals.

breechcloth—A Native American garment that covered the thighs and groin.

buckskins—Clothing made from the tanned hide of a male deer.

Bureau of Indian Affairs—The government agency that tries to help Native Americans make the best use of their land and resources.

cradleboard—A board or frame used by a Native American mother to carry a baby on her back. Wrappings bound the baby tightly to the cradleboard.

flash flood—A sudden, powerful flood, usually caused by a heavy rain.

Great Divide—A series of North American mountain ridges from which rivers flow westward on the western side and eastward on the eastern side.

interpreter—Someone who translates one language into a second language.

jerky—Meat that Native Americans preserved by drying thin strips in the sun.

journal—A written record of events, often kept on a daily basis.

keelboat—A riverboat built for carrying freight. In Lewis and Clark's day, keelboats could be sailed, rowed, poled, or towed.

laudanum—A form of opium that was used as a painkiller in the 1800s.

lodge—A general name for a wilderness shelter.

maize—A type of corn raised by Native Americans.

moccasins—The soft leather shoes made popular by Native Americans.

peace pipe—A highly decorated pipe that Native Americans used in their ceremonies.

pirogue—A large canoe made from a hollowed-out log.

pitch—A waterproof resin that Native Americans obtained from pine trees.

poultice—A soft, moist cloth that is used to treat an aching or inflamed part of the body. In the 1800s, poultices were often soaked in herbal preparations.

reservation—Land set aside by the government for the use of a Native American tribe.

scalps—Portions of the skin and hair cut from human heads as battle trophies.

tipi—A portable dwelling used by some Native Americans. A typical tipi consisted of a conical framework of poles covered with skins.

travois—A frame slung between trailing poles and pulled by a dog or horse. Native Americans used the travois to transport their belongings.

weaning—The process of training a baby to take nourishment other than by suckling.

wickiup—A frame hut covered with bark or brush.

yucca—A stiff-leaved, stemless succulent, native to Mexico and the western United States. Native Americans found many uses for the long fibers produced by the yucca's leaves.

MORE GOOD READING ABOUT
SACAGAWEA

Burt, Olive. *Sacajawea*. New York: Franklin Watts, 1978.

Clark, Ella E., and Margot Edmond. *Sacagawea of the Lewis and Clark Expedition*. Berkeley: University of California Press, 1979.

DeVoto, Bernard, ed. *The Journals of Lewis and Clark*. Boston: Houghton Mifflin Company, 1953.

Hebard, Grace R. *Sacajawea*. Glendale, Calif.: Arthur H. Clark Company, 1957.

Howard, Harold P. *Sacajawea*. Norman: University of Oklahoma Press, 1971.

Ronda, James P. *Lewis and Clark Among the Indians*. Lincoln, Neb.: University of Nebraska Press, 1984.

Schultz, James Willard. *Bird Woman (Sacajawea), the Guide of Lewis and Clark*. Boston: Houghton Mifflin Company, 1918.

Skold, Betty. *Sacagawea: The Story of an American Indian*. Minneapolis: Dillon Press, 1977.

INDEX